ETCHINGS BY
JIM DINE

NANCY OUTSIDE
IN JULY

TEXT BY
CLIFFORD ACKLEY

Copyright © 1983 ULAE
Published by ULAE
5 Skidmore Place
West Islip, New York 11795
U.S.A.

Library of Congress Catalog Card Number
83-50927
ISBN 0-910435-05-7

ACKNOWLEDGEMENTS

Seven years ago, Jim Dine worked for the first time at the legendary printshop of Aldo Crommelynck in Paris, creating four mysteriously beautiful etchings, prophetically titled *Paris Smiles*. The series that is the subject of this exhibition, *Nancy Outside in July*, was started in 1977 and finished in 1981. In the interim, it became clear that Dine—one of the preeminent graphic artists of our time—had surpassed even himself. We were quite overwhelmed, therefore, to learn that the Art Institute would receive a complete set of the twenty-five etchings as a gift from Jim Dine and Aldo Crommelynck. Moreover, the exhibiting museums would be able to offer their visitors a catalogue published by Universal Limited Art Editions, a name synonymous with the highest standards of printing. Clifford S. Ackley, who had written a penetrating essay on one of the *Nancy* prints when it was released, agreed to contribute the text for the catalogue. John A. Lund of Universal Limited Art Editions spent many painstaking hours on the technical analysis of this extraordinarily complex series. We are deeply grateful to Nancy Dine—Jim's wife and muse—for her "meditation" on the art of being a model. We are further indebted to Jim for lending a large group of unique proofs to the exhibition, so that we may share more fully in the joys of his creation.

Esther Sparks
Associate Curator of Prints and Drawings
The Art Institute of Chicago

These twenty-five pictures of my wife are her as I knew her from 1978 thru 1981.
She is my muse.

My collaborator for these works is the French printer, Aldo Crommelynck.
He is so much greater than any other in the world that to call him Printer is all that is necessary.

Nancy's friend and my friend Pep Crommelynck (Mrs. Aldo), is and was always with us during those heavy etching years in Paris.

Of course Nancy (herself) is the reason for the prints.

JIM DINE

Jim and Nancy Dine in their London studio.
Photograph by Edward Thordén.

Jim Dine and Aldo Crommelynck in the courtyard of Atelier Crommelynck.
Photograph by Nancy Dine.

Les vingt-cinq versions du portrait de sa femme Nancy éxécutées par Jim Dine entre 1978 et 1981 doivent être considérées comme un ensemble éminent, inséré dans une contribution à la gravure qui occupe une place importante dans son oeuvre. On peut y mesurer en raccourci l'étendue de sa maîtrise d'un art qu'il a pratiqué très tôt et dont il a dans sa jeunesse, obéissant à son tempérament, brusqué l'apprentissage. (brûlé les étapes d'apprentissage). Débutant impétueux, il reconnait avec une justesse prémonitoire que l'eau-forte—technique la plus apte à révéler la spontanéité—est la manière qui épanouira d'abord sa sensibilité. Puis, poursuivant sa conquête des procédés de la gravure, il en découvre les caractéristiques, les ressources expressives, et les soumet tous à l'autorité de sa vision. Guidé par son culte du naturel et de la liberté, autant que par son impatience innée, il aura tôt fait de dominer les exigences du métier et de s'affranchir complètement de la technique. De l'oeil à la main, de la sensation à la transcription, rien ne vient désormais entraver l'expression. Acuité du regard et sûreté de main exceptionnelle font naître une gravure vive et brillante, spirituelle et allusive qui n'admet pour règle que le caprice du peintre. La rapidité d'éxécution devenue principe de style, Jim Dine use d'une technique réinventée comme élément même de la création, comme terrain d'inspiration, avec ce don, si rare en gravure, de dessiner toujours du premier jet. L'insistance du thème de cette suite de vingt-cinq estampes souligne l'originalité d'une vision qui fonde son écriture sur la concision, sur l'abréviation. La verve de Dine s'exprime ici avec une entière liberté de facture, en volontaires et nettes affirmations, en notations aiguës qui montrent à la fois la puissance de son génie lapidaire—marque irrécusable—et que sans l'intervention patente d'une subjectivité, le métier n'est rien.

Aldo Crommelynck.

Jim Dine and Aldo Crommelynck in the courtyard of Atelier Crommelynck.
Photograph by Nancy Dine.

The twenty-five versions of the portrait of his wife, Nancy, executed by Jim Dine between 1978 and 1981 should be considered as a major suite, part of a contribution to printmaking that occupies an important place in his oeuvre. It serves as a summary of the scope of his mastery of an art that he practiced very early. In his youth, following his intuition, he was quick to learn (consuming the experimental stages). An impetuous beginner, he realized with premonitory accuracy that etching—the technique most suited to reveal spontaneity—was the first medium to expand his sensibility. Then, following his mastery of engraving methods, he discovered its characteristics, its expressive resources, submitting them all to the authority of his vision. Guided by his respect for the natural and for freedom as well as by his innate impatience, he was soon in command of the demands of the craft and was able to break away completely from the technique. From eye to hand, from feeling to transcription, from now on nothing would impede expression. Sharpness of sight and sureness of hand gave birth to lively, brilliant printmaking, spiritual and allusive, whose only rule was the whim of the artist. The speed of execution became the principle of his style. Jim Dine used a reinvented technique even as an element of creation, as a field of inspiration, with this gift, so rare in printmaking, of always being able to draw at the first attempt. The insistence of the theme of this suite of twenty-five prints stresses the originality of a vision that establishes his hand in conciseness, in brevity. Dine's energy is expressed here with a complete freedom of composition, with willing and distinct affirmations, in notations that show both his power and his genius in cutting. Without the obvious intervention of subjectivity, craft is nothing.

Aldo Crommelynck.

NANCY OUTSIDE
IN JULY

SITTING

Years ago, when these portraits were begun, it was much easier for me to look at them. I could easily answer questions like: "But why does he make your ears so red?" with a simple "Look at them, they really are." Now, however, twenty-five pictures later, I stand back and see a series of complicated, innovative portraits; pictures which consciously impress and dazzle me but, quite truthfully, terrify me at the same time.

The model sits but the artist observes. These observations are a public statement which is available to all who care to look. The internalization, the relationship between artist and model is a subject which has had many a person speculating. While we would all like to know if Mmes Matisse or Cézanne or any of the well-known models of Picasso had particular feelings about that part of their lives, very little information is available, I once read about Annette Giacometti, sitting in a cafe and asking her husband "Why are you staring at me?" and being extremely puzzled by the answer "Because I haven't seen you all day," as she had, in fact, been sitting for him all that day....Perhaps that is one tiny clue to the complicated relationship between artist and model.

It is tempting to think that one is inspiration. It is more realistic to think that it isn't necessarily *you* ...the physical and emotional elements one brings to the act of sitting are probably not those of the artist. The feeling and emotions expressed belong to him (or her) and ultimately, to the viewer.

There are advantages and disadvantages to almost everything one does including *sitting to be looked at*: For me, the advantages include the pleasure of seeing the creative process at work; the knowledge that can be gained both artistically and technically by observation and the intimacy and intensity of spending that time together. The disadvantages are the inability to ever divorce yourself from the fact that you are looking at a picture of you...and even though it's not a mirror, somehow you can't help thinking it is. Then, too, there is a moment when you are aware that the artist is concentrating on your left cheekbone...you can actually feel the brush or pencil on your face...it is at that moment that it begins to itch.

Nancy Dine, July 1982

I.

NANCY OUTSIDE IN JULY I

Edition of 60, plus 13 artist's proofs
White wove paper, watermarked ARCHES/FRANCE
23 × 19½ in. (plate); 35-5/8 × 24-7/8 in. (sheet)
Signed in pencil: 7/60 Jim Dine 1978

PLATE II.
Aquatint background. Printed in green.

PLATE III.
Skintones, aquatint with spitbite. Printed in flesh.

PLATE I.
Line drawing, soft ground and etching. Printed in black.

Eyes and lips painted in watercolor.

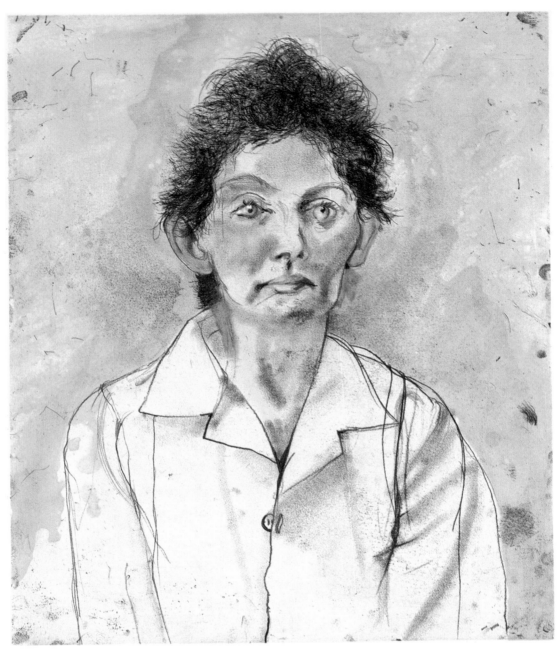

II.

NANCY OUTSIDE IN JULY II
Edition of 9, plus 4 artist's proofs
Cream mulberry (Kozo) paper, no watermark
23 × 19½ in. (plate); 35-5/8 × 24-1/8 in. (sheet)
Signed in pencil: 7/9 Jim Dine 1978

PLATE I.
Line drawing. Printed in black.

III.

NANCY OUTSIDE IN JULY III
Edition of 60, plus 10 artist's proofs
White wove paper, watermarked BFK RIVES/FRANCE
23 × 19½ in. (plate); 41½ × 29½ in. (sheet)
Signed in pencil: 7/60 Jim Dine 1978

PLATE I State 2.
Collar burnished out. Flowers added by softground drawing with
subsequent additions in drypoint and roulette. Printed in black

PLATE II.
Printed in black.

IV.

NANCY OUTSIDE IN JULY IV
Edition of 15, plus 10 artist's proofs
White wove paper, watermarked BFK RIVES/FRANCE
23 × 19½ in. (plate); 41½ × 29-7/8 in. (sheet)
Signed in pencil: 7/15 Jim Dine 1978

PLATE I State 2.
Printed in cold black.

PLATE II
Printed in black.

Additions of enamel paint in many colors.

PLATE I State 3.
Drypoint added to lower left corner.
Printed in warm black.

V.

NANCY OUTSIDE IN JULY V
Edition of 25, plus 10 artist's proofs
Cream mulberry paper (Kozo), no watermark
23 × 19½ in. (plate); 35-3/4 × 24 in. (sheet)
Signed in pencil: Jim Dine 1978 7/25

PLATE I State 4.
Highlights added to the hair by scraping and burnishing.
Plant leaves in neck area removed.
Printed in red-brown (conté).

Jim Dine 1978   7/25

VI.

NANCY OUTSIDE IN JULY VI:
FLOWERS OF THE HOLY LAND
Edition of 25, plus 6 artist's proofs and 4 unique proofs
Cream wove paper, watermarked ARCHES/FRANCE
23 × 19½ in. (plate); 35-3/4 × 24-7/8 in. (sheet)
Signed in pencil: 7/25 Jim Dine 1979

PLATE I State 5.
Addition of seed pods, large lilies, etc. in soft ground,
drypoint and burnishing. Printed in black.

Addition of enamel paint, thinned with turpentine.

PLATE I State 5.
Reprinted in black.

VII.

NANCY OUTSIDE IN JULY VII
Edition of 25, plus 6 artist's proofs and 1 unique proof
White wove paper (Rives), made for Crommelynck, no watermark
23 × 19½ in. (plate); 29-3/4 × 22¼ in. (sheet)
Signed in pencil: Jim Dine 1980
Inscribed by Crommelynck in pencil: 7/25

PLATE I State 6.
Additions in etching, soft ground and drypoint with
some scraping and burnishing. Flowers at ear level reinforced with burin.
Foul biting in upper right and left corners. Printed in black.

Addition of watercolor and wax crayon.

PLATE I State 6.
Reprinted in black.

7/25

VIII.

NANCY OUTSIDE IN JULY VIII
Edition of 14, plus 4 artist's proofs
Grey wove paper, watermarked BFK RIVES/FRANCE
23 × 19½ in. (plate); 29-3/4 × 22-1/4 in. (sheet)
Signed in pencil: 7/14 Jim Dine 1980

PLATE I State 6.
Printed in black.

7
14

1980

IX.

NANCY OUTSIDE IN JULY IX:
MARCH IN PARIS (TULIPS)
Edition of 22, plus 6 artist's proofs
White wove paper, no watermark
23 × 19½ in. (plate); 29-3/4 × 22-1/4 in. (sheet)
Signed in pencil: 7/22 Jim Dine 1980

PLATE I State 7.
Addition of aquatint over the entire plate. New flowers (tulips) added by
drawing with lithographic crayon on the aquatint before etching.
Addition of drypoint lines in area of flowers. Printed in black.

Additions of oil pastel and watercolor.

PLATE I State 7.
Reprinted in black.

X.

NANCY OUTSIDE IN JULY X:
YOUNG AND BLUE
Edition of 25, plus 7 artist's proofs
Buff wove paper, watermarked Arches
23 × 19½ in. (plate); 30 × 22-3/8 in. (sheet)
Signed in pencil: 7/25 Jim Dine 1980

PLATE I State 8.
Image partially effaced with buffing wheel, leaving weakened image of
previous work. Printed in brown.

PLATE III.
Printed in rose.

PLATE I State 8.
Printed in blue-green.

PLATE I State 9.
Addition of soft ground drawing altering nose, chin and shoulder lines.
Printed in blue-green.

PLATE II State 2.
Etched line drawing of hair, face, neck, and shirt added to the
existing background aquatint. Printed in black.

Thinned blue-green etching ink painted on both sides of the neck.
Blue-white ink applied under chin area.

XI.

NANCY OUTSIDE IN JULY XI: RED SWEATER IN PARIS

Edition of 25, plus 7 artist's proofs
White wove paper (Rives), made for Crommelynck, no watermark
23 × 19½ in. (plate); 29-3/4 × 22-1/8 in. (sheet)
Signed in pencil: 7/25 J Dine 1980

PLATE II State 2.
Printed in turquoise.

PLATE I State 9.
Printed in black.

Addition of buff, flesh and blue on face; red on sweater; and
green on neck; in acrylic paint.

PLATE I State 9.
Reprinted in black.

PLATE IV.
Reused from the etching *Paris Smiles,* 1976[1].
Printed in black.

Addition of tan splatter in acrylic paint over face.

(1) *Jim Dine Prints: 1970-1977.* Published in association with
Williams College Artist-in-Residence Program. Catalogue by
Thomas Krens et. al. Harper & Row, Publishers, N.Y., 1977.
Catalogue 218 reproduced.

XII.

NANCY OUTSIDE IN JULY XII: GREEN LEAVES
Edition of 30, plus 8 artist's proofs
White wove paper, watermarked BFK RIVES/FRANCE
23 × 19½ in. (plate); 41-7/8 × 29-5/8 in. (sheet)
Signed in pencil: Jim Dine 1981
Inscribed by Crommelynck in pencil: 7/30

PLATE V.
Sugarlift and aquatint with spitbite, printed in green.

PLATE II State 2.
Printed in blue.

PLATE III.
Printed in flesh.

PLATE II State 2.
Printed in black.

PLATE VI.
Thin etched lines added to hair, eyes, nose, mouth, and ears.
Gestural outlines of face, neck, and torso, and crosshatches through torso.
Printed in black.

PLATE VII.
An impression of Plate 1, State 9, was photographed and a half-tone
silkscreen made. This image then silkscreened on a copper plate and etched.
Printed in light grey.

PLATE I State 9.
Printed in black.

PLATE I State 9.
Reprinted in black.

XIII.

NANCY OUTSIDE IN JULY XIII:
DISSOLVING IN EDEN
Edition of 30, plus 10 artist's proofs
White wove paper, watermarked BFK RIVES/FRANCE
23 × 19½ in. (plate); 30 × 22¼ in. (sheet)
Signed in pencil: Jim Dine 7/30 1980

PLATE VII.
Printed in black.

PLATE VII.
Selectively inked in the face only. Printed in pink.

PLATE II State 2.
Printed in turquoise.

PLATE IV.
Reversed and printed in yellow.

PLATE I State 9.
Printed in black.

XIV.

NANCY OUTSIDE IN JULY XIV: WRESTLING WITH SPIRITS

Edition of 30, plus 9 artist's proofs
White wove paper, watermarked BFK RIVES/FRANCE
23 × 19½ in. (plate); 36 × 25 in. (sheet)
Signed in pencil: Jim Dine 1981
Inscribed by Crommelynck in pencil: 7/30

BLANK PLATE:
Inked in cobalt blue, printed as background.
This plate is ½ inch larger in both dimensions than the other plates used.

PLATE VIII.
A variation of Plate VII made with the same
silkscreen used in making Plate VII.

PLATE IX.
Heavy line drawing of hair, cowl at neck, outlines of arms and shoulders,
done with electrically vibrated drypoint. Printed in black.

PLATE I State 9.
Printed in blue-grey.

PLATE II State 2.
Printed in grey.

PLATE I.
Printed in black.

XV.

NANCY OUTSIDE IN JULY XV: NANCY OVER THE TREES

Edition of 15, plus 6 artist's proofs
White wove paper (Arches), no watermark. The "paper" used was an
unpublished variant edition of a 1981 etching of a tree, which had been
printed in black, and white, and again in black.
23 × 19½ in. (plate); 40-3/4 × 34-5/8 in. (sheet)
Signed in white crayon: 7/15 Jim Dine 1981
Plate area painted in white acrylic.

PLATE X.

An impression of Plate I, in a working state between States 1 and 2,
was photographed and used to make a photogravure plate which
became the basis of Plate X. This photogravure etching was altered
with electric burnishing tool and electrically vibrated drypoint,
changing areas in the face, shoulder lines, sides of the
neck, collar, and background. Printed in black.

Selective brushing of white acrylic paint over parts of the painted image.
White oil pastel highlights added to face.

XVI.

NANCY OUTSIDE IN JULY XVI:
JAPANESE BISTRE
Edition of 19, plus 6 artist's proofs
Ivory oatmeal paper, no watermark
23 × 19½ in. (plate); 36½ × 26-5/8 in. (sheet)
Signed in pencil: 7/19 J. Dine 1981

PLATE XI.
A drawing on frosted mylar was photographically transferred to a
copper plate using the dichromated gelatin resist process of photogravure.
This process was published in:
Deli Sacilotto, *Photographic Printmaking Techniques.*
New York, Watson-Guptill Publications
1982, pages 127-138, reproduced pages 131-135.
Printed in brown.

XVII.

NANCY OUTSIDE IN JULY XVII:
THE REDDISH ONE
Edition of 26, plus 6 artist's proofs
Grey wove paper, watermarked BFK RIVES/FRANCE
23 × 19½ in. (plate); 29-7/8 × 22-1/8 in. (sheet)
Signed in pencil: 7/26 J. Dine 1981

PLATE VII.
Printed in Rubine Red.

PLATE X.
Printed in Rubine Red.

XVIII.

NANCY OUTSIDE IN JULY XVIII:
FULL OF EXPRESSION
Edition of 15, plus 4 artist's proofs
White wove paper, watermarked BFK RIVES/FRANCE
23 × 19½ in. (plate); 36 × 24-3/4 in. (sheet)
Signed in pencil: 7/15 J. Dine 1981

PLATE XI.
Printed in black.

Addition of oil pastel colors.

PLATE XI.
Reprinted in black.

PLATE I State 9
Printed in black.

XIX.

NANCY OUTSIDE IN JULY XIX:
THE FISH IN THE WIND

Edition of 25, plus 6 artist's proofs
White wove paper, watermarked BFK RIVES/FRANCE
23 × 19½ in. (plate); 29-7/8 × 22 in. (sheet)
Signed in white crayon: J. Dine 7/25 1981
Paper is painted in black acrylic

PLATE I State 9.
Printed in white.

PLATE V State 2.
Additions to plate by electrically vibrated drypoint in the area of the plants.
Highlights burnished on plant leaves. Printed in white.

PLATE VI.
Printed in white.

Moe   7/25   1981

XX.

NANCY OUTSIDE IN JULY XX:
AMONG FRENCH PLANTS
8 artist's proofs
White wove paper, watermarked BFK RIVES/FRANCE
23 × 19½ in. (plate); 29-7/8 × 22 in. (sheet)
Signed in pencil: Jim Dine 1981 A/P

PLATE XII.
Sugarlift and aquatint, with tonal highlights made with
electric burnishing tool. Printed in black.

PLATE III.
Skin tones printed in light orange

PLATE XIII.
The photograph used to make Plate X was used to make a new
photogravure plate. Brush drawing added either to the photograph or
(by sugarlift or solvent lift) to the photogravure plate.
Tonal highlights added with electric burnishing tool. Printed in black.

XXI.

NANCY OUTSIDE IN JULY XXI: THE RED FRAME

Edition of 22, plus 4 artist's proofs
Cream wove paper, watermarked ARCHES/FRANCE
23 × 19½ in. (plate); 35-7/8 × 24-7/8 in. (sheet)
Signed in pencil: Jim Dine 7/22 1981

PLATE XIII.
Printed in black.

PLATE XIV.
A drawing of Nancy, from life, was made into a rubber stamp,
which was then rolled with sugarlife and "printed" on a metal plate.
This plate was etched and printed in the conventional way. Printed in black.

Light blue acrylic paint was brushed over the entire plate area.
A red acrylic paint border was painted around the blue, using
the plate mark as a guide.

PLATE XIII.
Reprinted in black.

Jim Dine   7/22   1981

XXII.

NANCY OUTSIDE IN JULY XXII: TEN LAYERS OF GREY
Edition of 28, plus 9 artist's proofs
White wove paper, watermarked BFK RIVES/FRANCE
23 × 19½ in. (plate); 36 × 25 in. (sheet)
Signed in pencil: Jim Dine 1981 7/28

PLATE VII.
Printed in grey.

PLATE II State 2.
Printed in grey-black.

PLATE VIII.
Printed in grey-black.

PLATE IX.
Printed in black.

PLATE VI.
Printed in black.

PLATE IX.
Reprinted in white.

PLATE XI.
Printed in white.

PLATE X.
Printed in grey-white.

PLATE I State 9.
Printed in black.

PLATE X.
Reprinted in black.

1981

XXIII.

NANCY OUTSIDE IN JULY XXIII:
SQUEEZED OUT ON JAPANESE PAPER
Edition of 25, plus 6 artist's proofs
Light brown mulberry (Chiri) paper with flecks, no watermark.
23 × 19½ in. (plate); 36 × 24½ in. (sheet)
Signed in pencil: Jim Dine 1981 A/P

PLATE XV.
The method used to transfer the rubber stamp to Plate XIV (in Print 21)
was used to make this plate. Printed in black.

XXIV.

NANCY OUTSIDE IN JULY XXIV:
BRILLIANT DUTCH GLOSS
Edition of 18, plus 4 artist's proofs
White wove paper, watermarked BFK RIVES/FRANCE
23 × 19½ in. (plate); 36 × 24-7/8 in. (sheet)
Signed in pencil: Jim Dine 1981 7/18

PLATE XVI.
Etched line and aquatint with burnishing and drypoint. An aquatint was
bitten over the entire plate. A drawing was scraped out of the
aquatint for a "mezzotint" effect in the face, neck, collar and arms,
and criss-crossing in the background. A line drawing was then etched
over this work with additional drypoint accents. Printed in grey.

Additions of enamel, thinned with turpentine, throughout.

PLATE I State 9.
Printed in black.

XXV.

NANCY OUTSIDE IN JULY XXV: CHARCOAL CYCLAMEN

Edition of 9, plus 2 artist's proofs
Cream wove paper, watermarked ARCHES/FRANCE
23 × 19½ in. (plate); 35-3/4 × 24-7/8 in. (sheet)
Signed in pencil: Jim Dine 7/9 1981

PLATE I State 9.
Printed in black.

PLATE III.
(Skin tones) printed in flesh.

Charcoal drawing of flowers in lower margins and within plate mark.

Zoe 7/9   1981

NANCY OUTSIDE IN JULY: A PORTRAIT IN TIME

When Jim Dine began work on the series of etchings of his wife, Nancy, in July 1977, he planned to etch a maximum of ten variant versions. When the last edition was signed in 1981, the series had grown to twenty-five etchings, characterized by a variety of approaches to intaglio print-making, an extensive use of multiple overprinting, and a great diversity in choice of paper. Many of the etchings also involved a generous use of overpainting or over drawing by the artist's hand, resulting in images that, although editioned, are essentially unique. This ambitious expansion of the original dimensions of the project is characteristic of Dine's restless energy and his appetite for pushing the media as far as they will go.

Like many other artists who emerged on the New York art scene in the late 1950s and early 1960s, Dine naturally gravitated to thinking in terms of serial imagery. Many of Dine's earliest prints, such as the *Car Crash* lithographs of 1960 or the *Ties* drypoints of 1961, were conceived as series or sets, as variations on a theme.

Always latent in printmaking is the potential for leaving a permanent record of the artist's thinking and creative process by means of impressions taken at different stages in the development of the plate or block or by means of variations in inking and papers. The first major print-maker to take full advantage of printmaking's potential for the permanent recording of the evolving image was Rembrandt van Rijn. The first state of his portrait of the industrious Dutch printseller and publisher Clement de Jonghe seems to be a direct notation from life: the sitter's features are clearly illuminated and their particularity stressed; his expression is neutral, impassive (Fig. 1). In the third state, however, shadow plays about the eyes and mouth, veiling their expression in ambiguity (Fig. 2). The broad-brimmed hat is also more generalized, less the portrait of a particular rumpled hat. The image is now as much a meditation on the mystery of human personality as it is the portrait of a specific individual.

(Fig. 1)
Rembrandt van Rijn. *Clement de Jonghe*. 1651. Etching, first state. Museum of Fine Arts, Boston. Harvey D. Parker Collection.

(Fig. 2)
Rembrandt van Rijn. *Clement de Jonghe*. 1651. Etching, third state. Museum of Fine Arts, Boston. William Francis Warden Fund.

(Fig. 3)
Edgar Degas. *The Engraver Joseph Tourny.* 1857.
Etching, printed in brown ink. Museum of Fine Arts, Boston.
Bequest of W. G. Russell Allen.

It was not until the mid- and later nineteenth century that larger numbers of artists took creative advantage of the evolving or variant image in printmaking. In two impressions of Edgar Degas' early etched portrait of his friend and instructor in the craft of etching, the engraver Joseph Tourny, one sees how radically Degas could transform an etched image by the manner in which he printed it (Figs. 3, 4). In the Boston impression of this veritable homage to Rembrandt, the lightly etched plate is printed traditionally, wiped clean of all excess printing ink; it is as delicate as a fifteenth-century Italian silverpoint drawing or a portrait by Ingres made with a hard pencil. In the New York impression Degas printed with printer's ink on the smooth surface of the copper plate as Rembrandt had done in certain impressions of his later etchings. This special inking evokes a tenebrous play of light and shadow that envelops Tourny in an aura of introspective mystery.

(Fig. 4)
Edgar Degas. *The Engraver Joseph Tourny.* 1857, probably printed 1870s.
Etching. The Metropolitan Museum of Art, New York.
Harris Brisbane Dick Fund.

(Fig. 5)
Félix Bracquemond. *Edmond de Goncourt.* 1882. Etching, first state.
Museum of Fine Arts, Boston. Samuel P. Avery Fund.

The printmaker's creative involvement with the evolving image is seen once more in the first and last states of the portrait of the writer, collector, and amateur artist Edmond de Goncourt, etched by Degas' friend the professional printmaker Félix Bracquemond (Figs. 5, 6). The objects that furnish the interior allude to Goncourt's interest in Japanese art and to his advocacy of the revival of eighteenth-century French art. The elegantly unfinished first state of the etchings is primarily concerned with silhouette and with a sinuous line that heralds Art Nouveau, while the final state is conceived tonally and charged with suggestion of color and texture. In the first state Goncourt is more haggard and anxious, in the last more sleek and complacent.

The serial imagery of *Nancy Outside in July* does far more than testify to printmaking's ability to provide a permanent record of the unfolding of the creative process. This series, in which Nancy Dine's image is restlessly transformed—one moment rosy, blooming, caressed by living flowers *(VII)*, the next transparent, wraith-like, peering through a screen of spectral roses *(XIX)*—forces the viewer to confront such fundamental issues as the cycle of living and dying or the many different personas that a single evolving personality may encompass in a lifetime.

The painter Georgia O'Keeffe touched upon the latter idea when, after many years, she once again examined the several hundred photographs that make up the many-faceted portrait in time which Alfred Stieglitz made of her from 1917 to 1937 (Figs. 7, 8). "When I look over the photographs Stieglitz took of me—some of them more than sixty years ago—I wonder who that person is. It is as if in my life I have lived many lives."[1]

Nancy Dine, in her concise, thoughtful meditation on "sitting" included in this book, has raised the pertinent issue of whether the particular individual who "sits" for the artist is to be identified with the image finally portrayed in the artist's work or is merely a representative human image, a springboard for the artist's visual imagination. The present series, however, is clearly labeled with Nancy's name.

(Fig. 6)
Félix Bracquemond. *Edmond de Goncourt.* 1882.
Etching, eighth and final state. Museum of Fine Arts, Boston.
Horatio C. Curtis Fund.

(Fig. 7)
Alfred Stieglitz. *A Portrait.* 1919.
Photograph, Palladium print. Museum of Fine Arts, Boston.
Gift of Alfred Stieglitz.

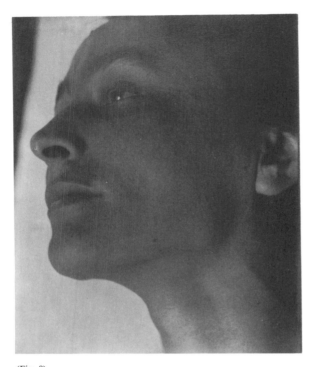

(Fig. 8)
Alfred Stieglitz. *A Portrait.* 1922.
Photograph, Palladium print. Museum of Fine Arts, Boston.
Gift of Alfred Stieglitz.

(Fig. 9)
Portrait of a Lady. Mummy portrait on wood panel.
Roman Egypt, 2nd century A.D.. Museum of Fine Arts, Boston.
Cheney and Everett Funds.

A number of the etchings have an ethereal, otherworldly aspect that seems to place them in an ambiguous realm outside the stream of time: Nancy's body takes on a ghostly transparency, there is uncertainty as to whether flowers spring up before her breast or within it *(XV)*. The prominence and luminosity of the eyes in many of the *Nancy Outside in July* etchings suggest the spiritual, otherworldly gaze of Roman sculpture of the Late Antique period or the mummy portraits painted in wax pigments on wooden panels from the Fayum region of Roman Egypt (Fig. 9).

Some literal-minded viewers may be shocked at the changes to which the artist has subjected Nancy's image and might be tempted to conclude that Jim and Nancy's relationship was a troubled one: in reality they are unusually close, virtually one person—a team. When wishing to make a point about the changes attendant on the stresses of living and time's inevitable erosions, Dine has not spared his own image. His 1974 *Dartmouth* self-portrait etchings were produced by sanding down a series of nine 1971 drypoint self-portrait plates and then reworking the faint traces of the initial conception, violently transfiguring them into images that make us acutely conscious of the skull beneath the skin. So shocked by this rather macabre metamorphosis, a curator who closely follows Dine's work was said to have recommended immediate psychotherapy for the artist. Dine's conscious transformation of his own image was not, however, an act of psychic irresponsibility but should rather be seen as part of a long tradition of memento mori imagery associated with the portrait. One thinks, for example, of those sixteenth-century northern European painted portraits in which the back of the wooden panel was decorated with a still life of skull and burnt-out candle. In other instances, the sitter even more blatantly holds a skull or points to one significantly and was thus constantly admonished by this explicit symbol of mortality to curb his or her pride and vanity.

In the *Nancy Outside in July* etchings, Nancy Dine's image is frequently associated with flowers. Nancy is caressed by flowers or obscured by them; she incorporates flowers into her body or wears them like a flowered kimono. In one print, Nancy's shock of hair mimics, dahlia-like, the petals of a flower (*XX: Among French Plants*). Flowers are, of course, traditional symbols of the fragile beauty and evanescence of life. A close identification of flowers and the portrait image occurred earlier in Dine's etched work in the playful 1974 series of self-portraits, *Self-Portraits in a Ski Hat* (Fig. 10), in which the artist wears a tulip-like ski cap and is gradually engulfed by tulips.

It will come as no surprise to the reader to learn that Nancy Dine is an avid gardener, loves flowers, and is interested in the history of botanical illustration. I remember visiting the Dines in Vermont last summer. A runaway flower garden tumbled down the hillside to the brink of the swimming pool. Beside the pool both Dines proudly pointed to a clump of rank Jack-in-the-beanstalk sunflowers that nodded far above our heads.

The 1971 drypoint self-portraits so dramatically transformed in 1974 are one of the earliest instances of Dine's new interest in the human face and figure. Prior to this, articles of clothing (ties, bathrobes) and tools often served as stand-ins or metaphors for the artist's own image or the parts of the human body. These objects were usually presented with a cool, if often sweet, "Pop" irony. Since the early seventies, however, Dine's prints, and, especially, his drawings of the human face and figure, are often so charged with raw feeling that such difficult-to-define terms as "Romantic" or "Expressionist" inevitably spring to mind.

Dine's near obliteration of the nine 1971 drypoint self-portraits before totally reworking them to produce the 1974 *Dartmouth* self-portraits has its parallel in the *Nancy* prints. Dine, at a certain point in the development of the Nancy plate, had the whole image ground down on a metalworker's buffing wheel in order to produce a more delicate image, literally a ghost of its former self. In a similar fashion, Dine, in his recent drawings, like van Gogh in his early drawings, uses a thick, sturdy paper chosen for its ability to stand up to his attack as he scrubs, gouges, and works into already executed surfaces with a

(Fig. 10)
Jim Dine. *Self-Portrait in a Ski Hat (Surrounded by Tulips)*. 1979. Etching, second state. Courtesy of Pace Editions.

(Fig. 10A)
Jim Dine. *Self-Portrait in a Ski Hat (Tulips)*. 1979. Etching, third state. Courtesy of Pace Editions.

variety of tools, including a rotary sander. Sometimes he goes right through the paper. These energetic physical attacks on plate and paper remind one of Dine's roots in New York School Abstract Expressionism or Action painting.

Dine's close give-and-take collaboration with the Parisian master printer Aldo Crommelynck has produced a set of prints of dazzling technical complexity. Not only was a broad spectrum of traditional intaglio techniques employed in the execution of the Nancy images; the master plate was also employed to generate further plates by means of silkscreen or photogravure transfer of the image to new printing plates. In one burst of technical invention, a rubber stamp was made from a drawing of Nancy, and the resulting image transferred under pressure of the press to an aquatint plate, a process literally and wittily alluded to in the title *Squeezed Out on Japanese Paper*. So complex are these procedures that even artist and printer have had difficulty in reconstructing precisely what was done and in what sequence.

It is often difficult to discuss the *Nancy Outside in July* etchings in terms of traditional printmaking because many of them are as much paintings or drawings as prints. The *Nancy* etchings are frequently translucent, layered images comparable in character to the translucent, veiled layers of a painting. This is the result not only of the application of colors by hand but also of successive overprintings from multiple plates as well as the intentional off-register reprinting of the same plate. The hand-applied color has usually been added between printings so as to seal it in and make it a more integral part of the image.

The modern roots of the hand-colored artist's print may be traced back to late nineteenth-century France to certain impressions of prints by Redon and Gauguin. In the twentieth century the tradition of the hand-colored print was continued by the German Expressionists, by Kirchner and Pechstein, among others. Dine has been involved with the hand-coloring of print editions from the early years of his printmaking career, as in the 1961 set of drypoint *Ties* (Fig. 11). In the 1970s the turn to hand-coloring of print editions or of individual prints on the part of artists and

(Fig. 11)
Jim Dine. *The Universal Tie*. 1961.
Dry point with watercolor. Museum of Modern Art, New York.
Leon A. Mnuchin Fund.

publishers signified—as did the new interest in handmade papers—a reaction against the crisp, fabricated perfection and sometimes sterile uniformity of many 1960s' print editions.

In the Nancy etchings, as in many of Dine's earlier prints, the choice of papers adds another dimension of color and texture. A good example is the etching referred to above, *XXIII: Squeezed Out on Japanese Paper*, a flecked, freckled image that has been printed on a similarly flecked, light brown Japanese mulberry paper. Here the paper supplies all of the color and much of the texture. It was the late Tatyana Grosman of Universal Limited Art Editions who first introduced Dine, as well as many other contemporary painter-printmakers who started out in the sixties, to the expressive potential of unusual handmade papers.

The twenty-five etchings that compose Jim Dine's *Nancy Outside in July* are a good deal more than yet another example of creative virtuosity in today's collaborative printmaking. They are simultaneously a moving demonstration of printmaking's ability to leave a permanent record of the image evolving in the artist's mind, a love letter, and a meditation on time.

CLIFFORD ACKLEY

(Fig. 11A)
Jim Dine. *Little Flesh Tie*. 1961.
Dry point with watercolor. Museum of Modern Art, New York.
Gift of Mr. and Mrs. Leon A. Mnuchin.

[1] Introduction to *Georgia O'Keeffe, A Portrait by Alfred Stieglitz*, The Metropolitan Museum of Art, New York, 1978.